THIS COLORING BOOK BELONGS TO

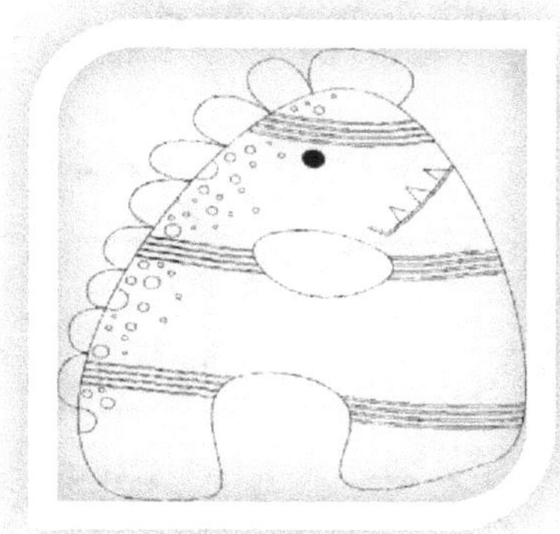
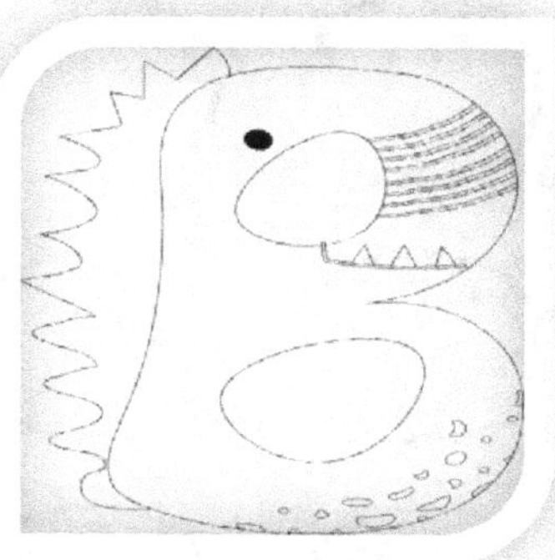
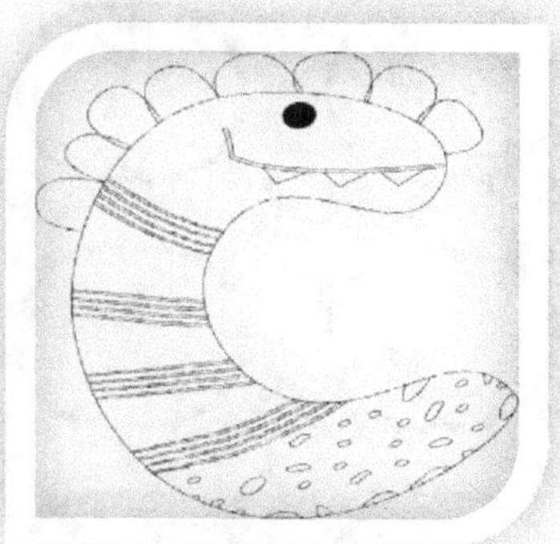

COLOR TEST PAGES

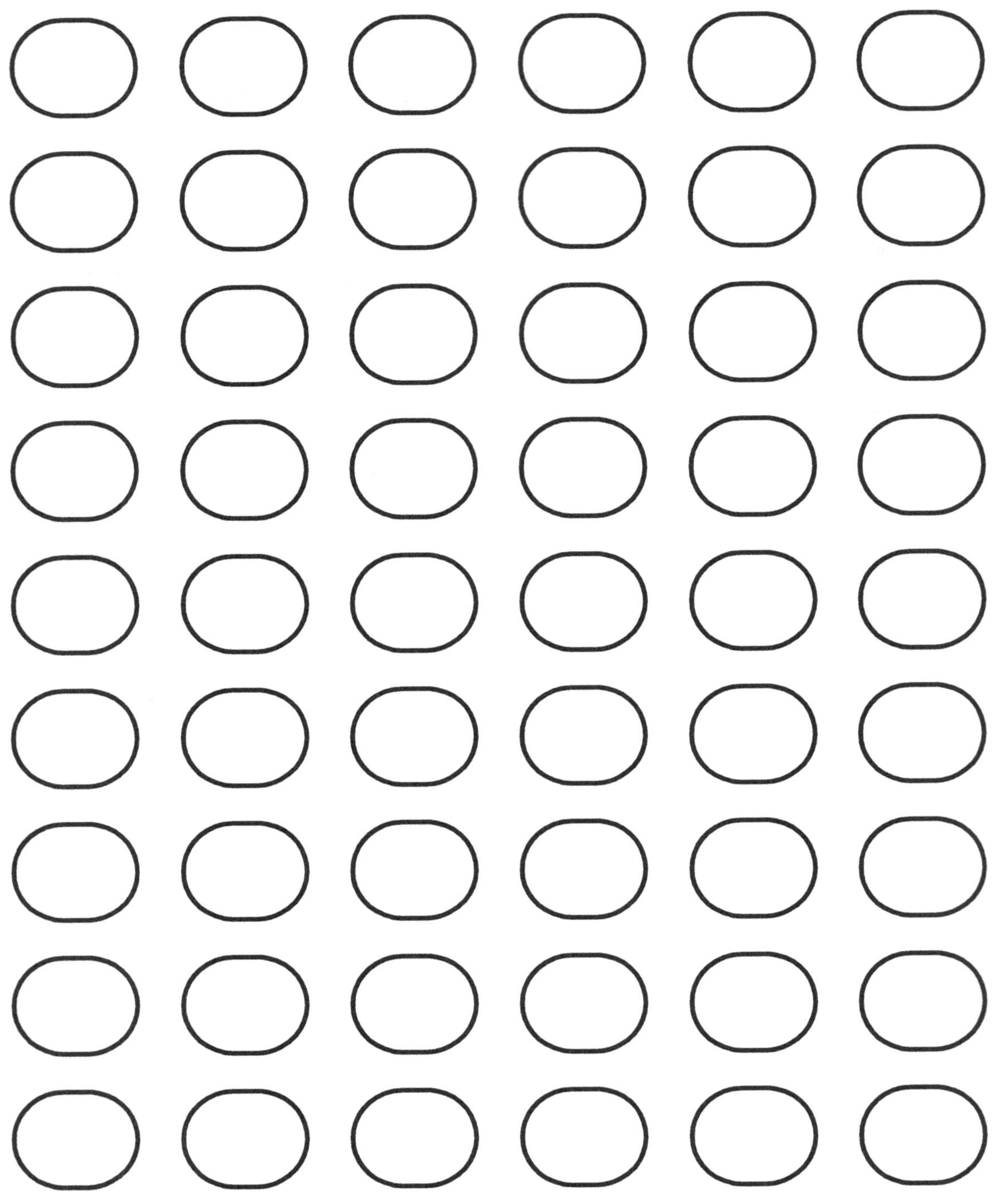

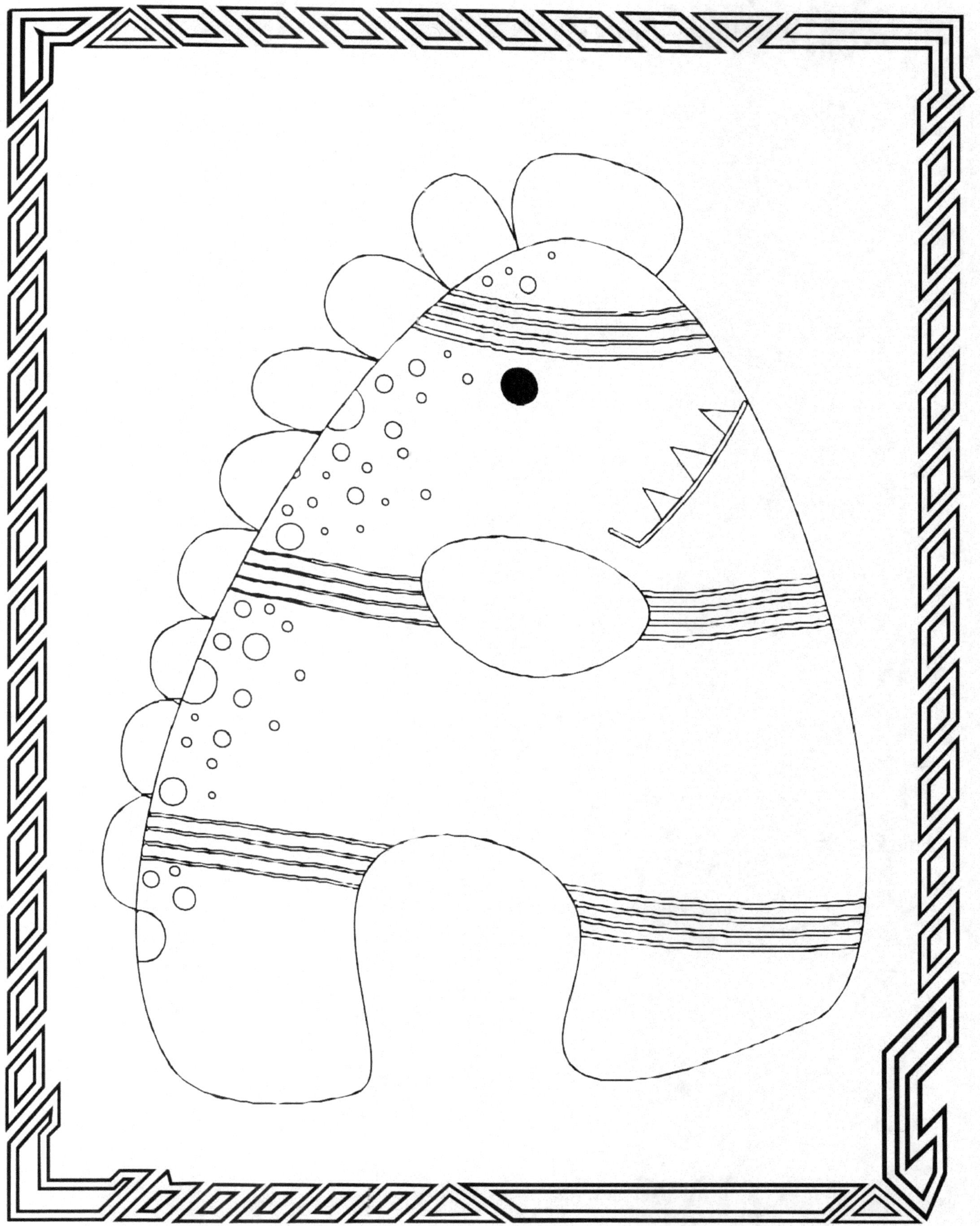

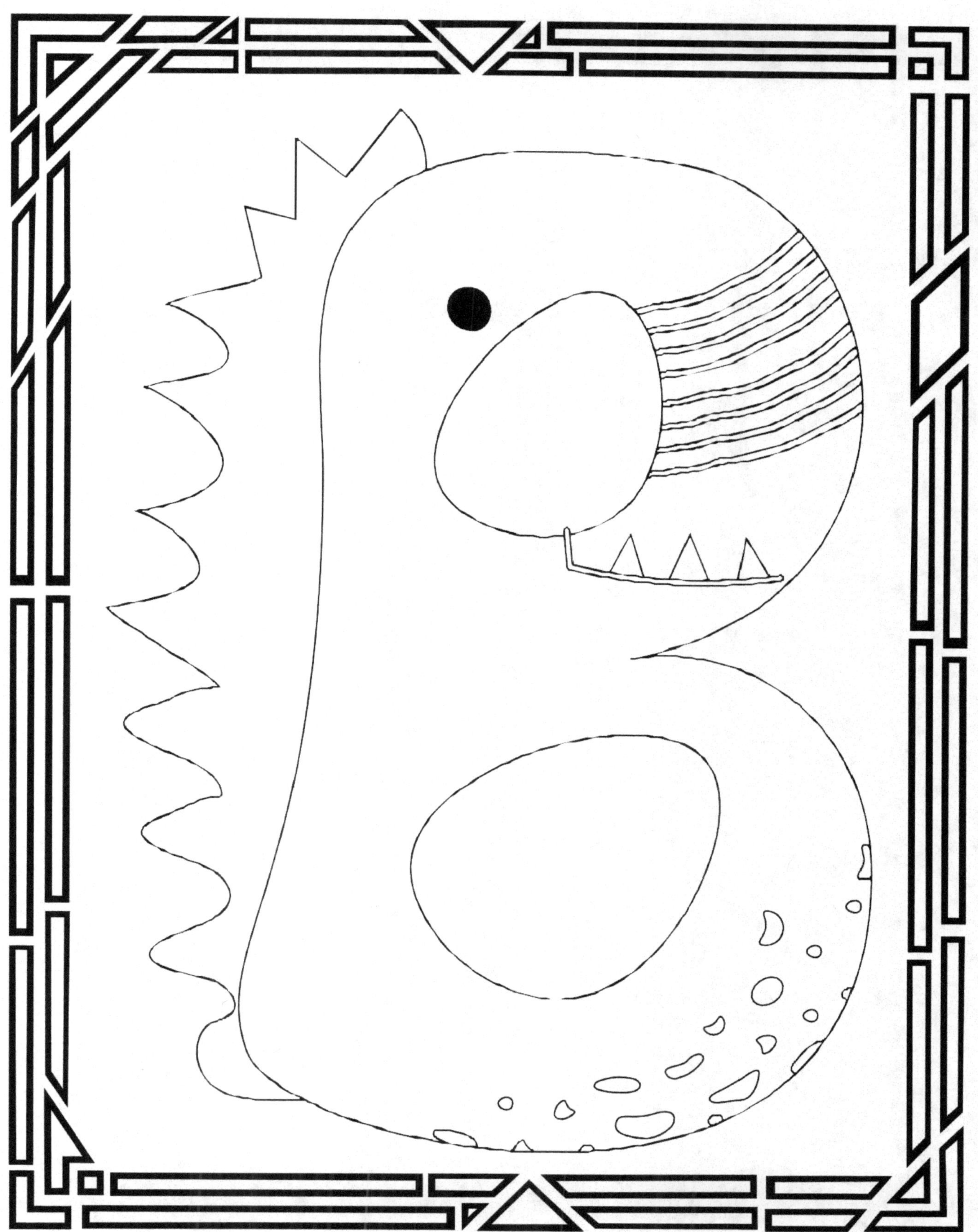

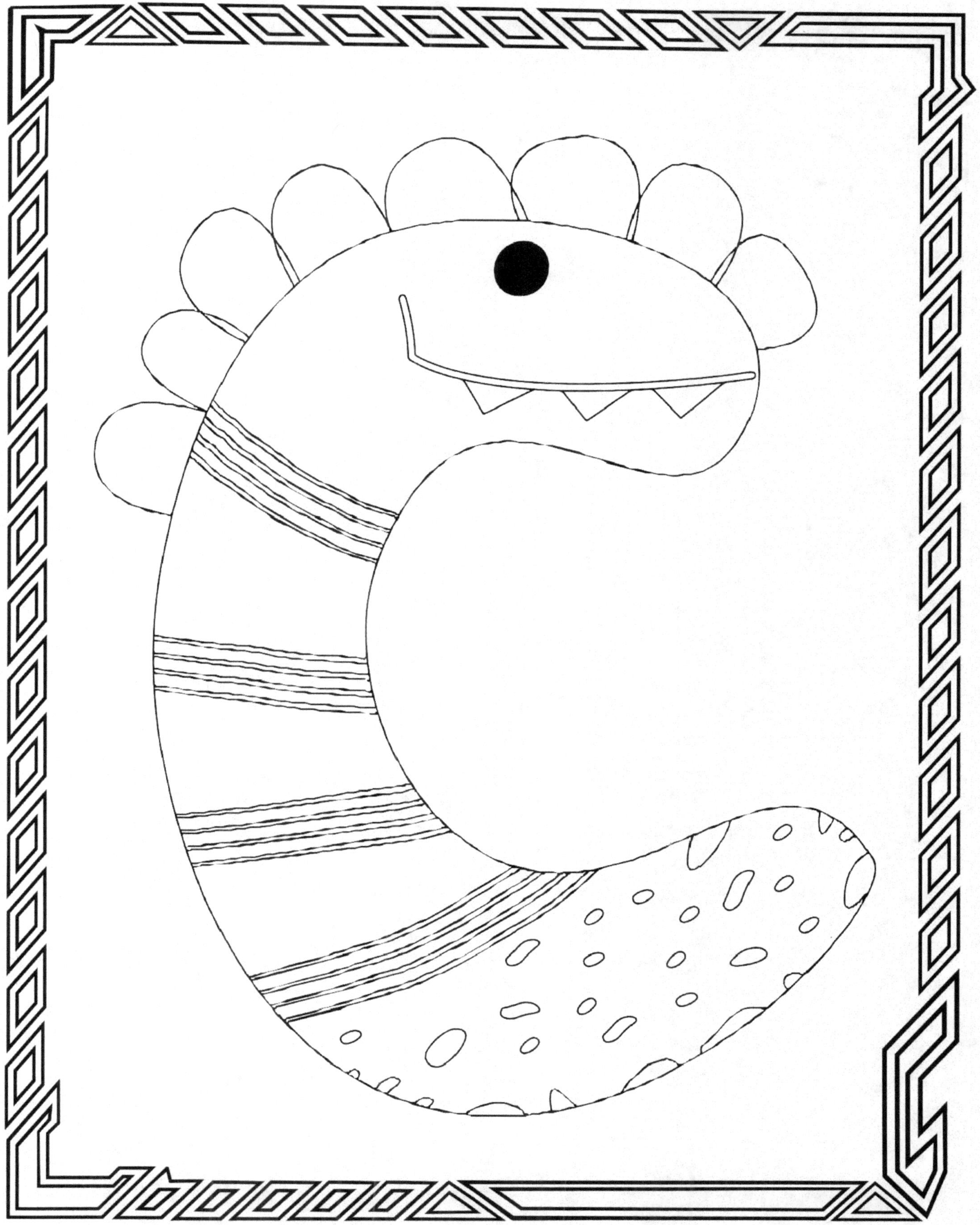

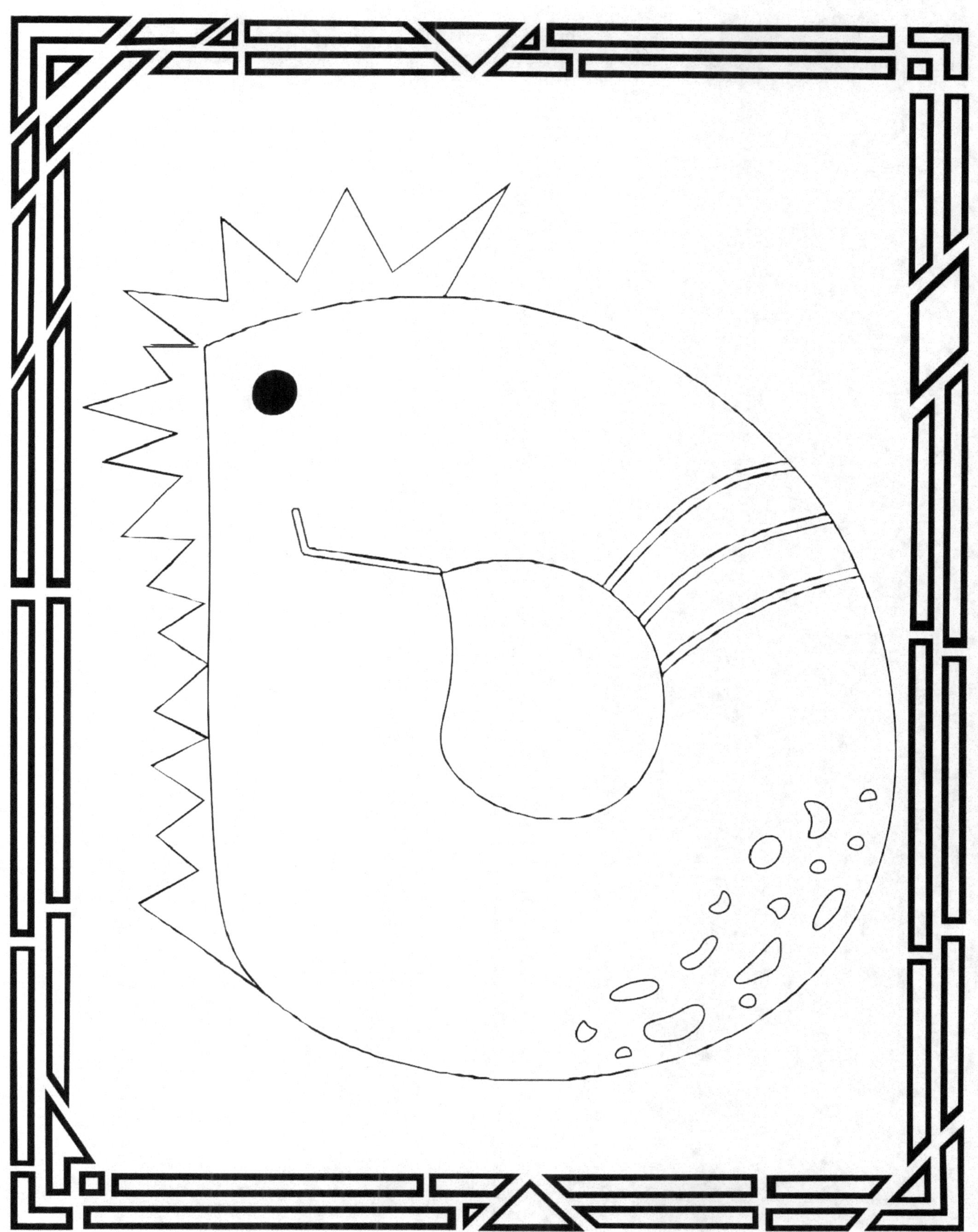

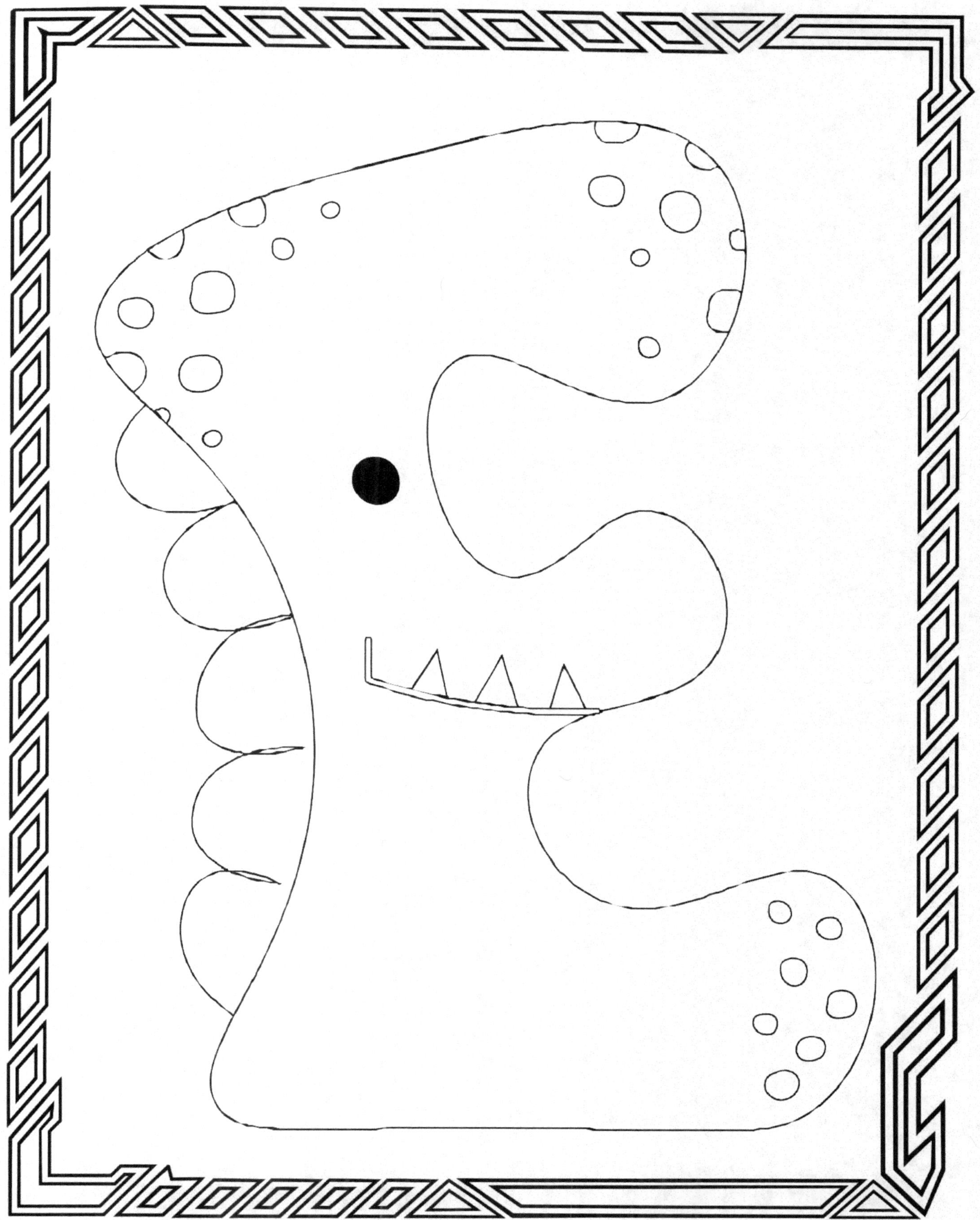

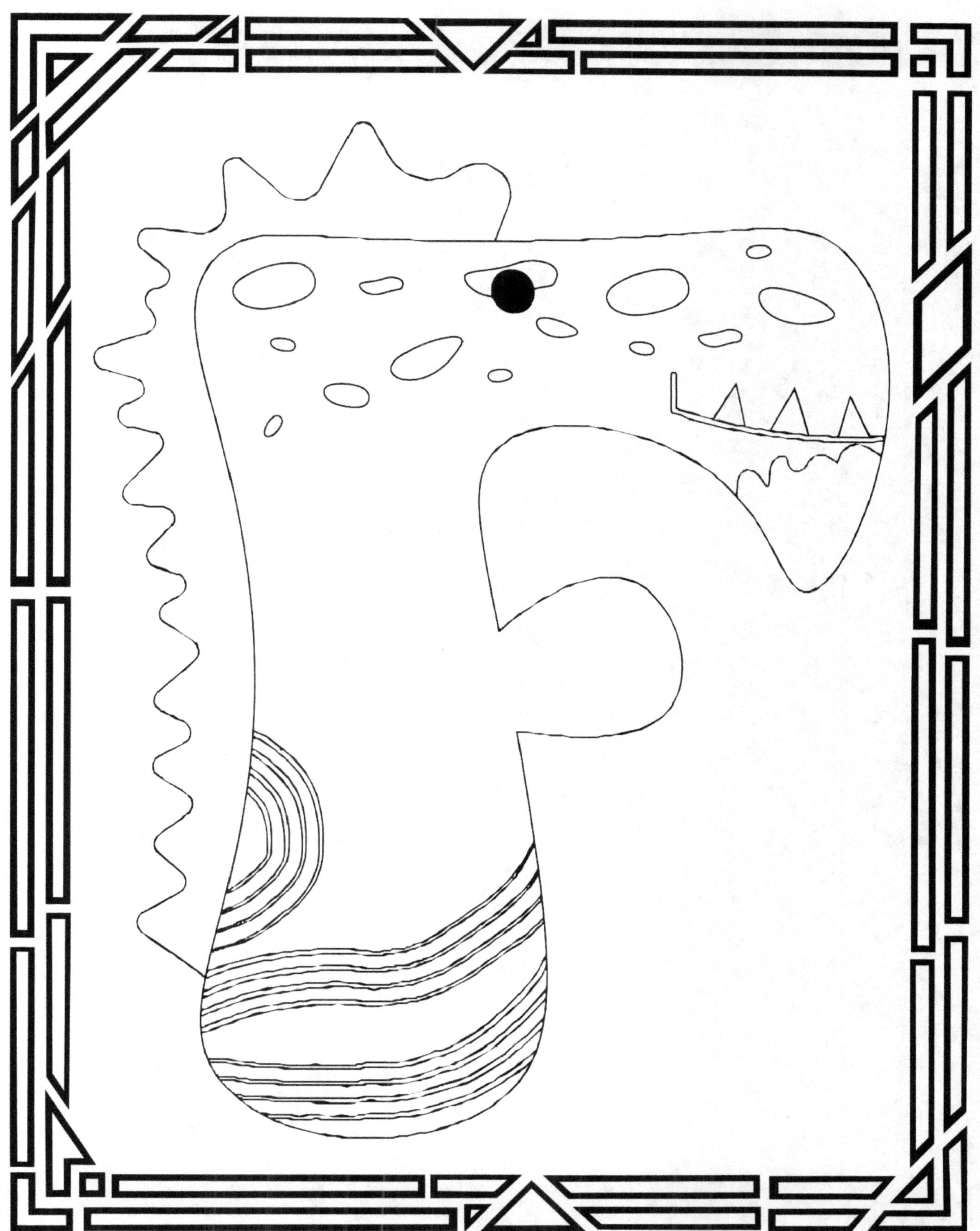

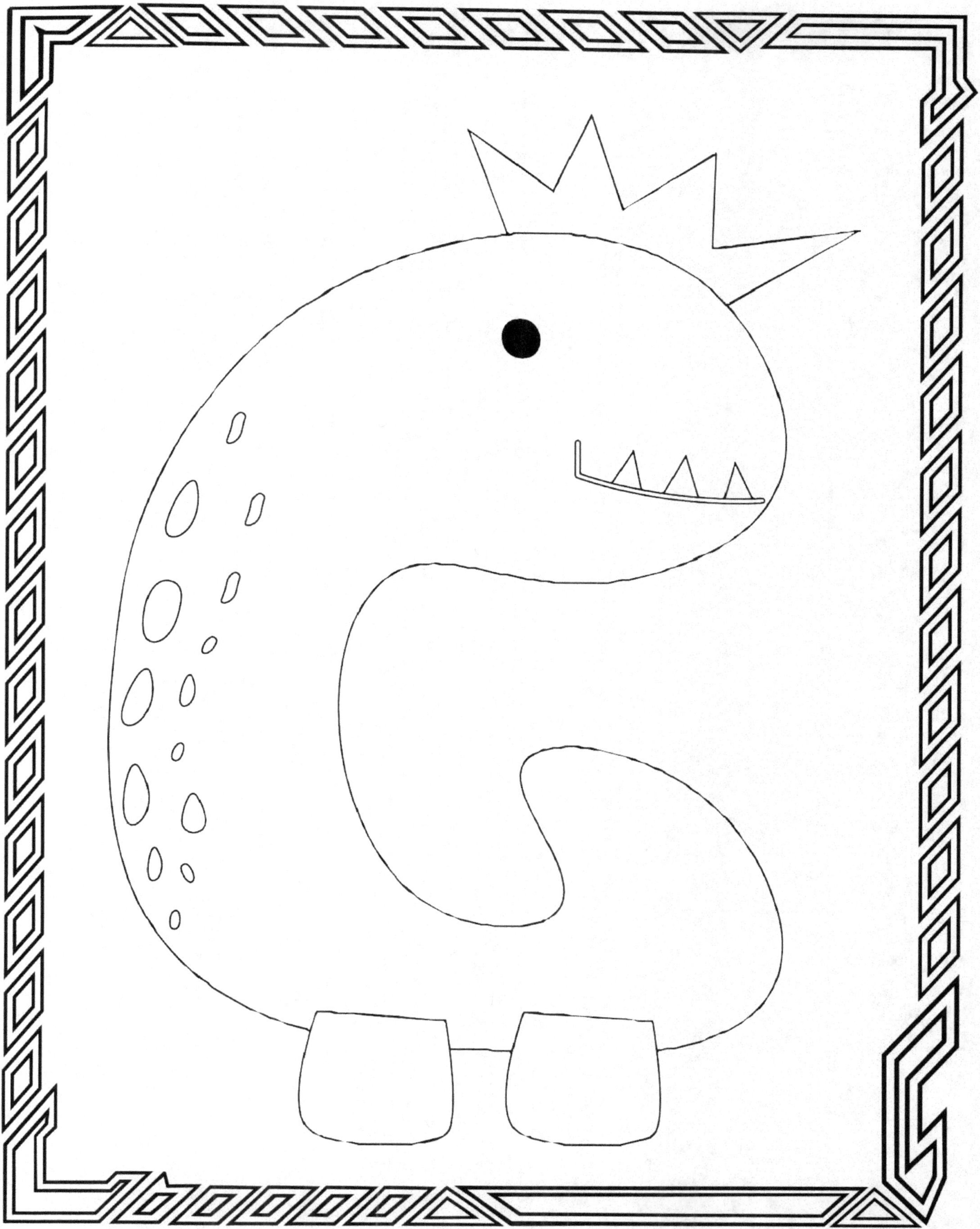

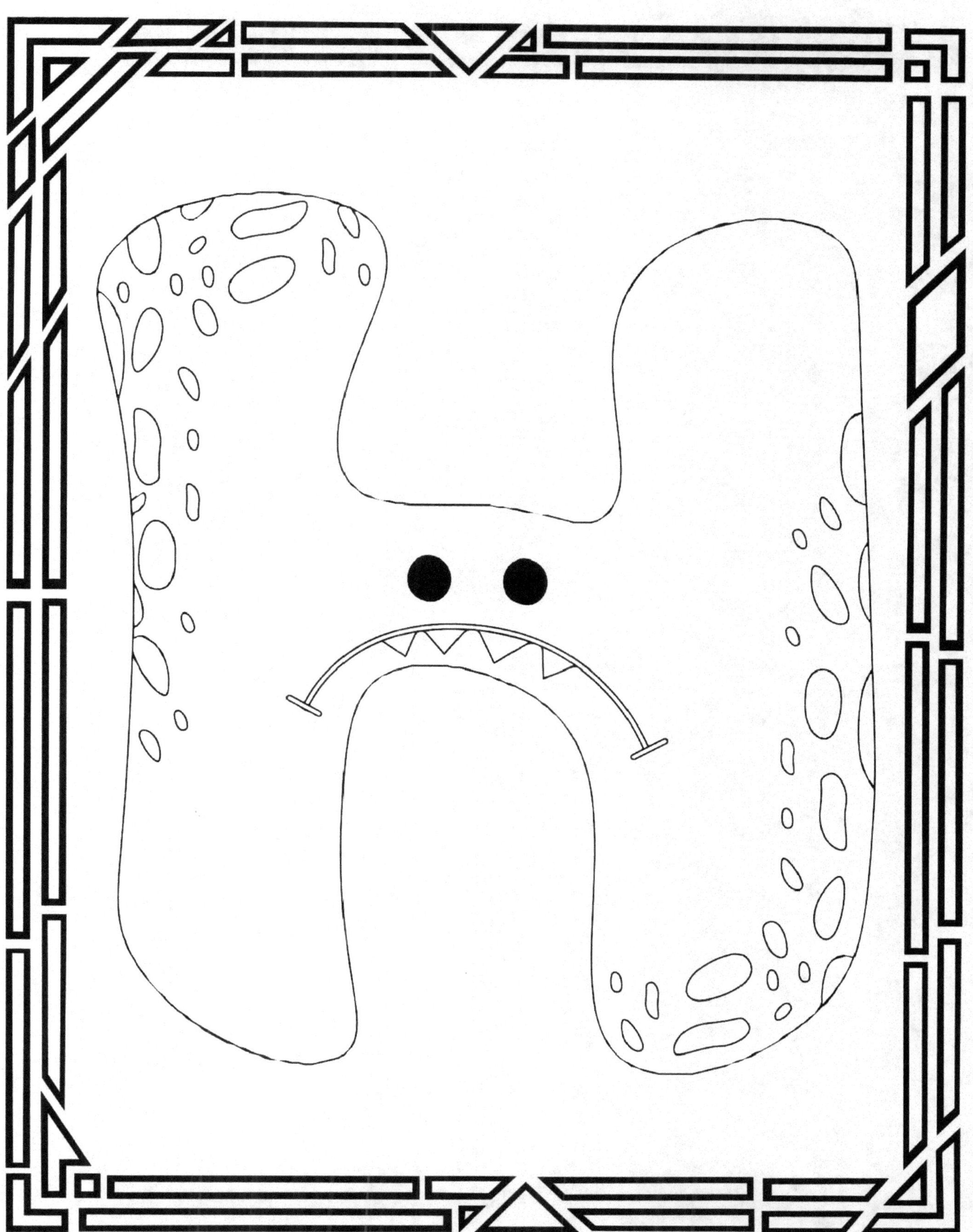

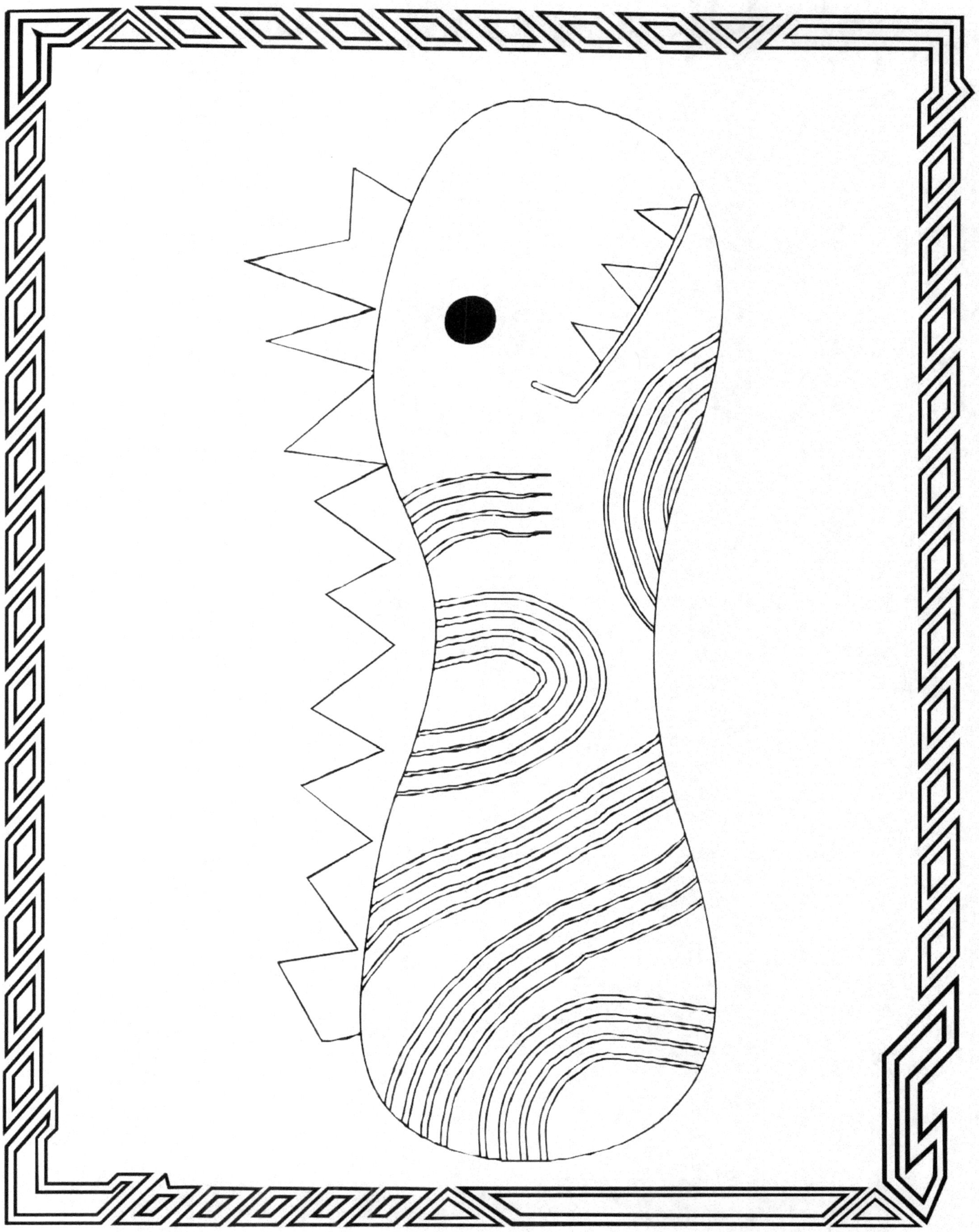

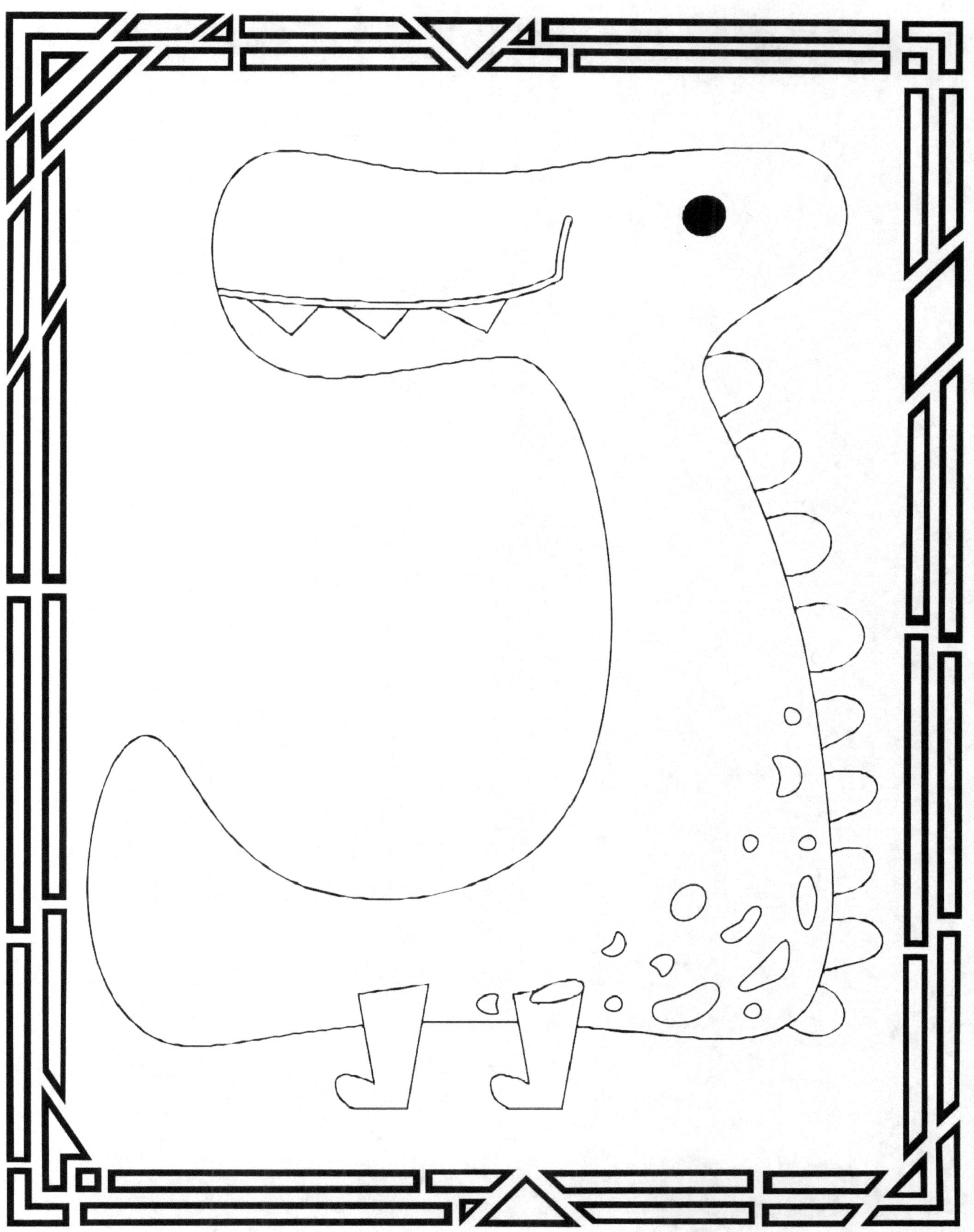

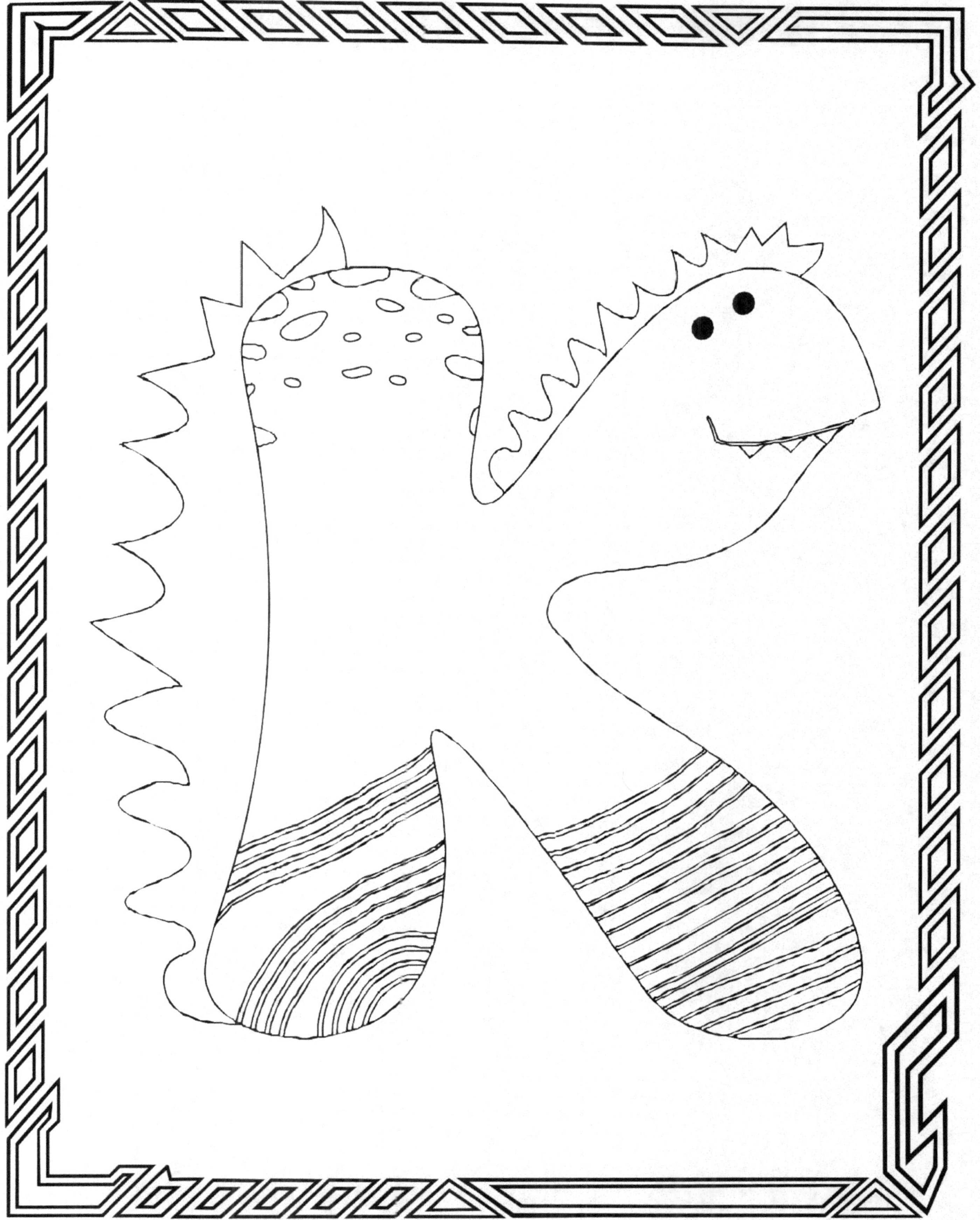

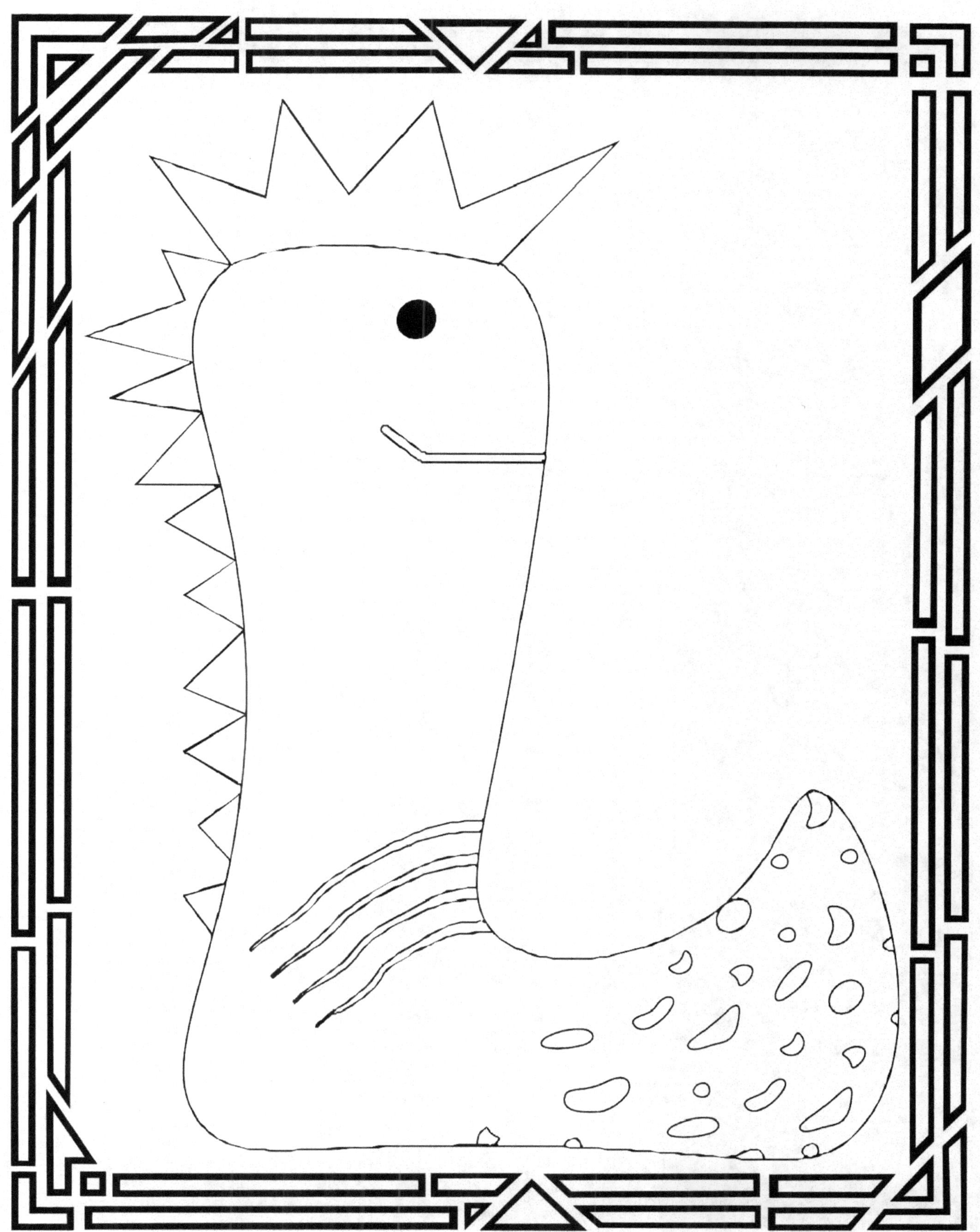

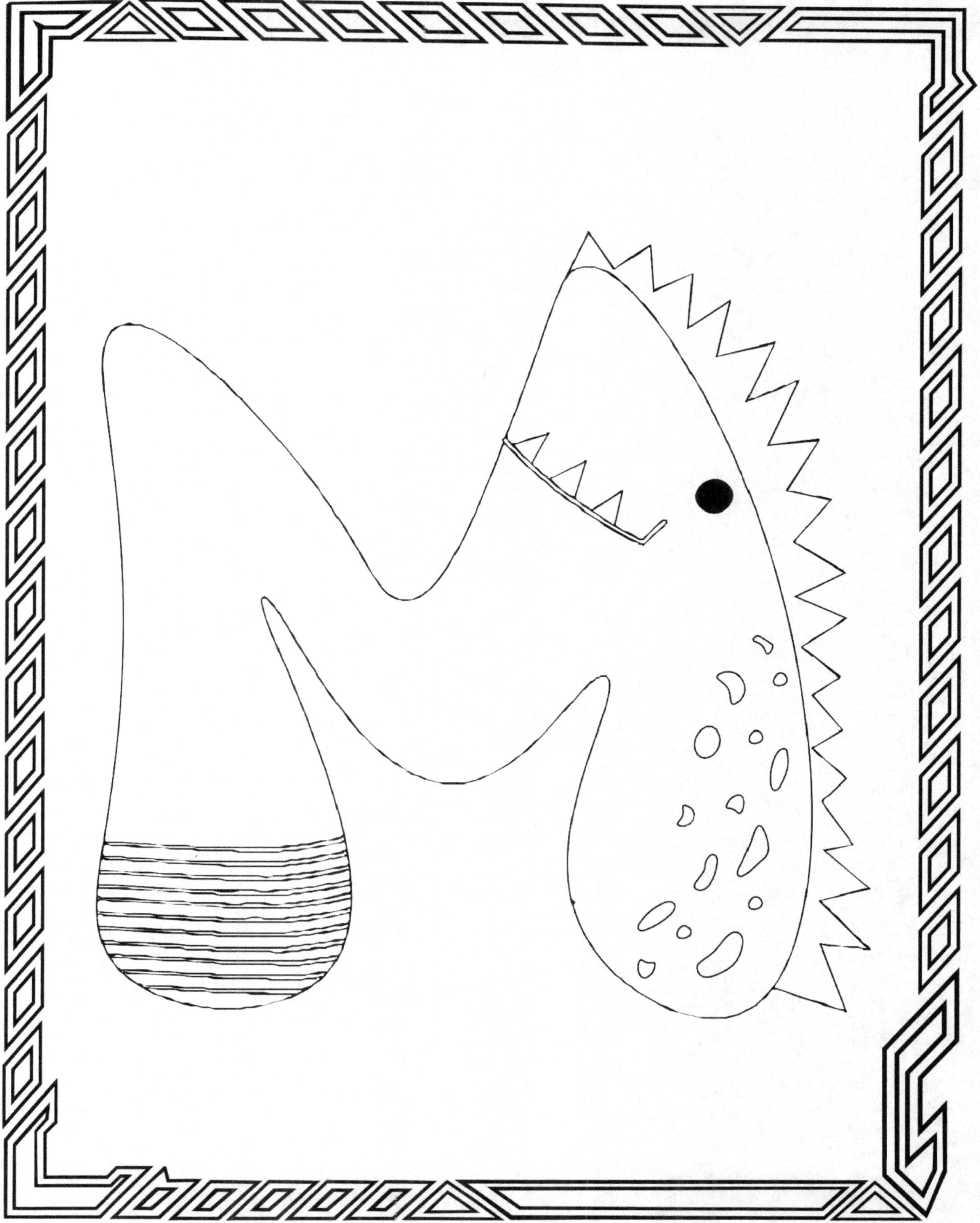

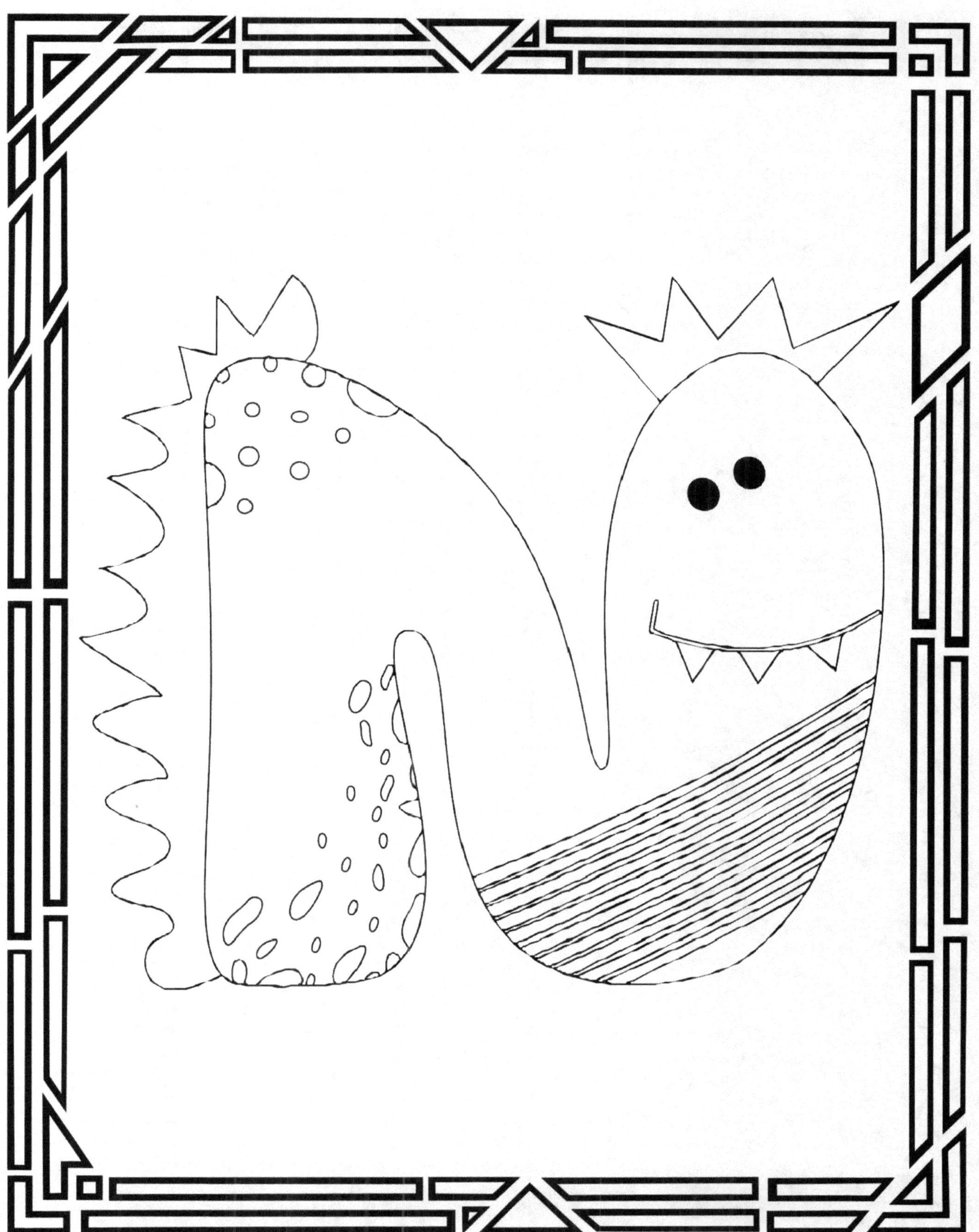

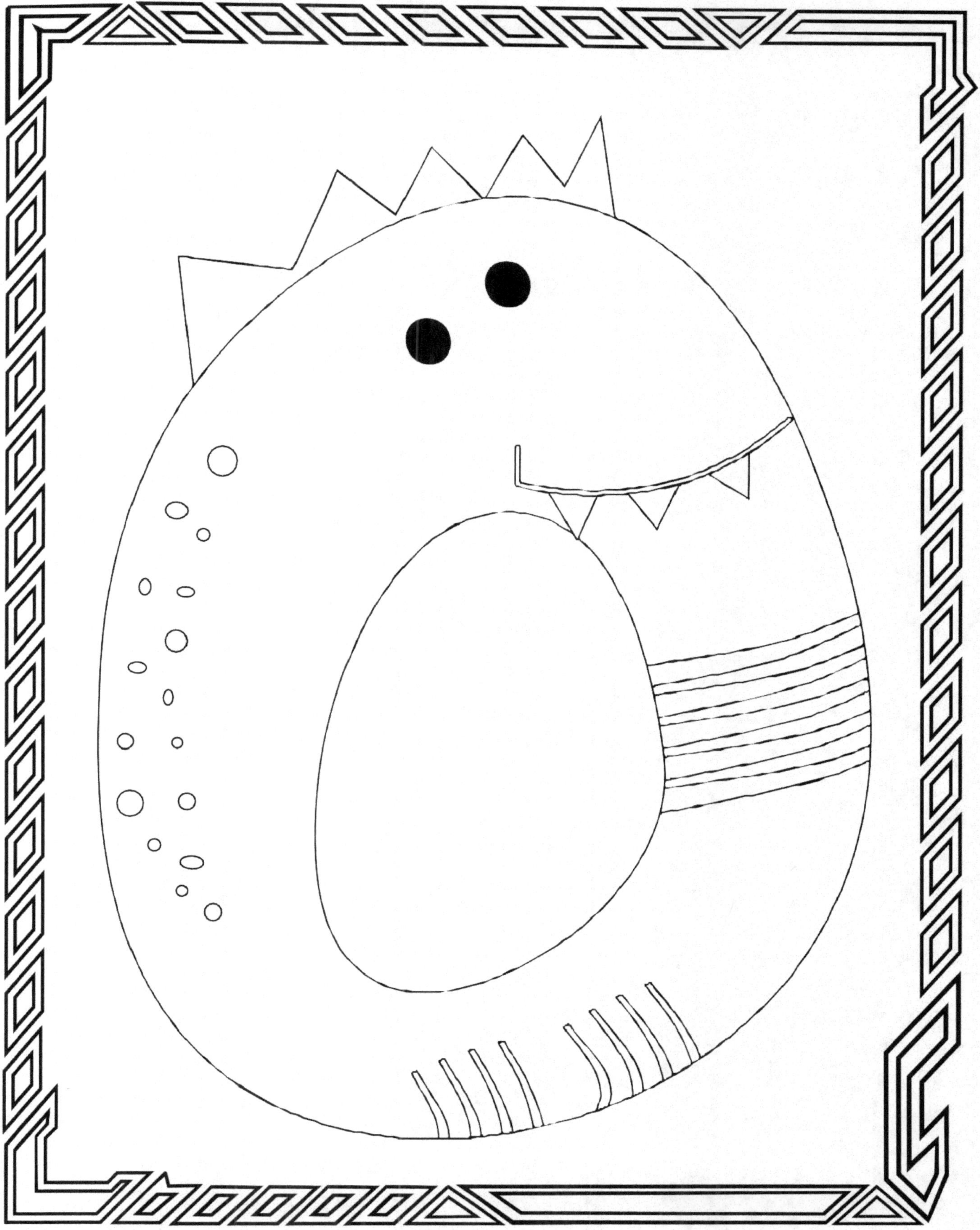

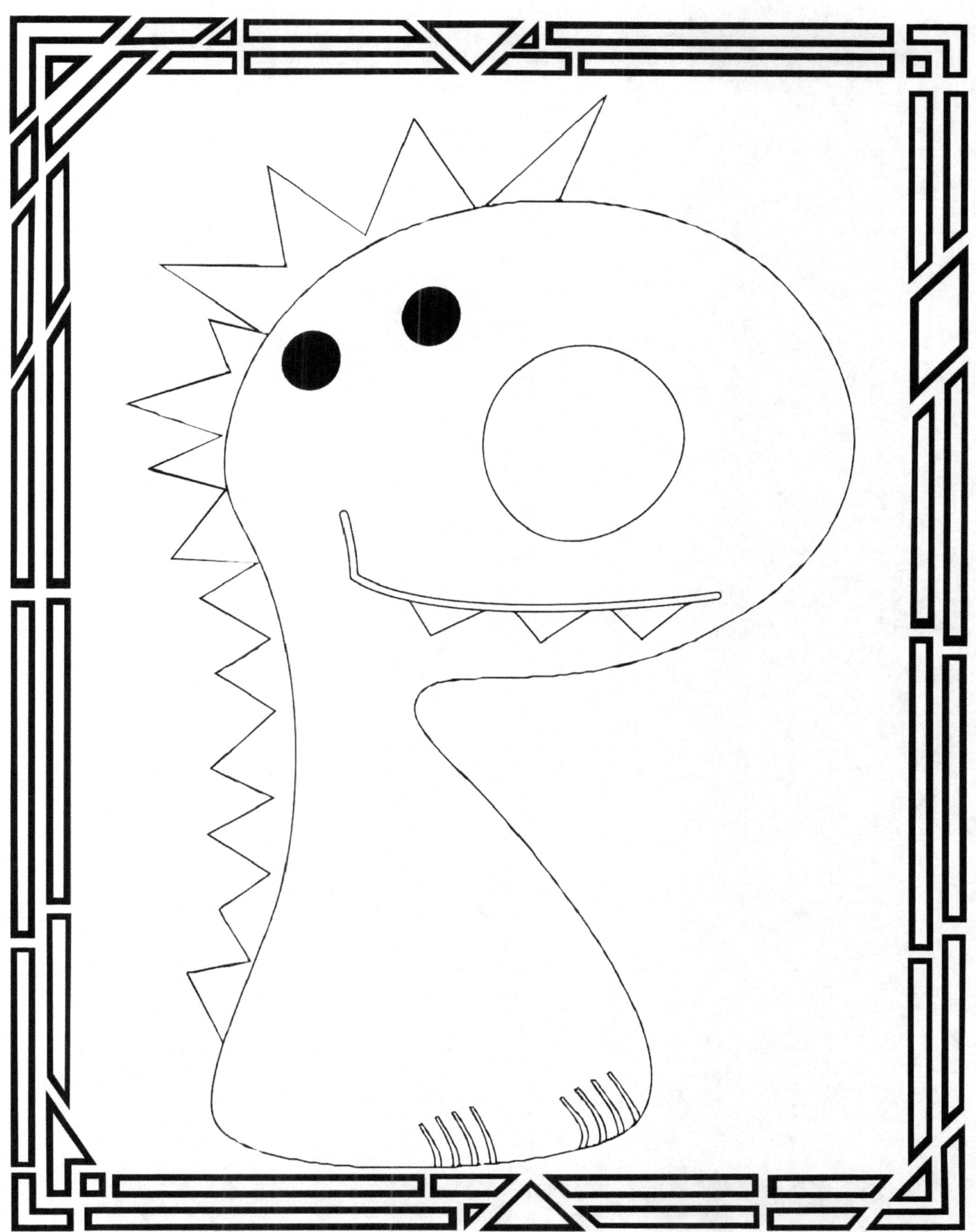

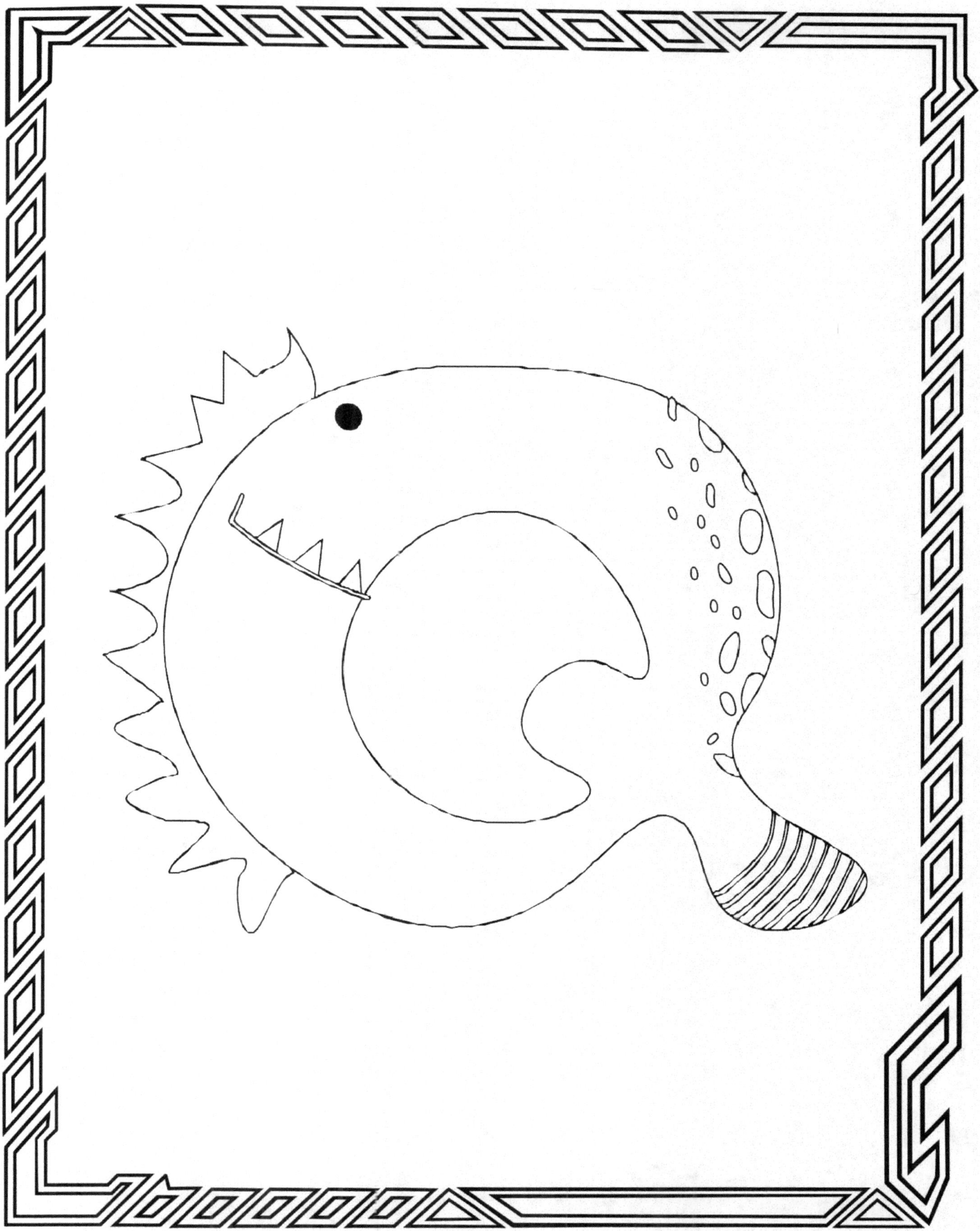

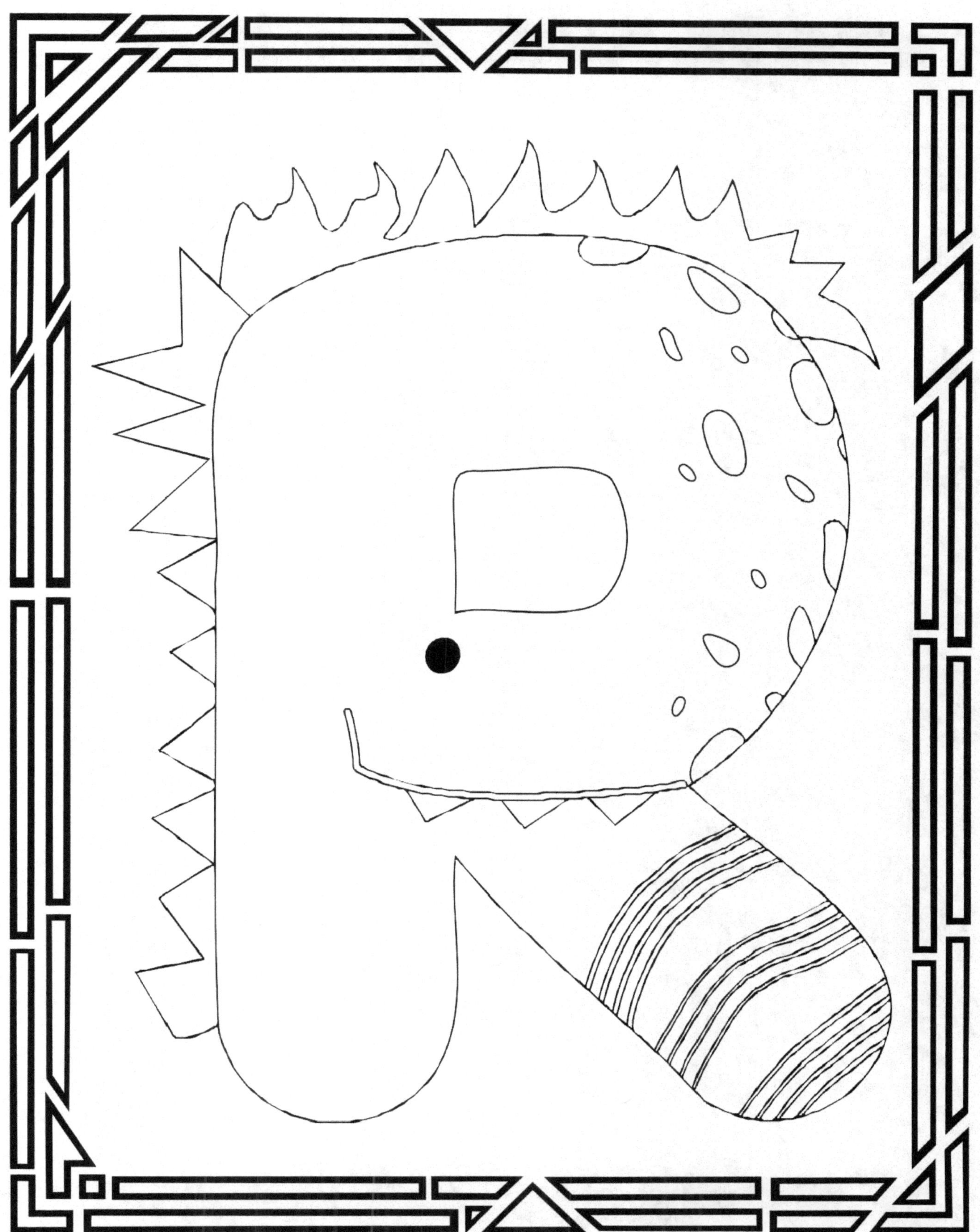

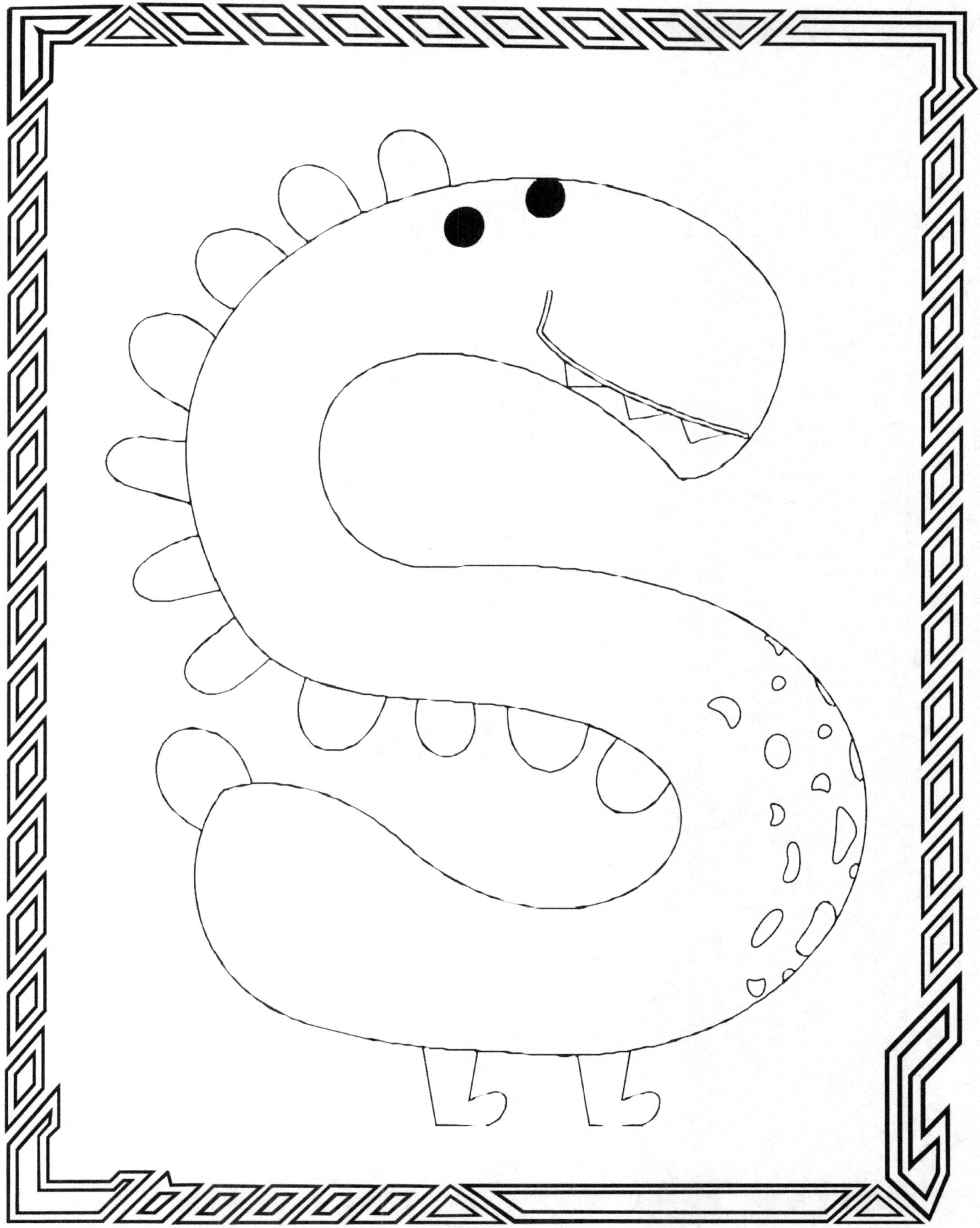

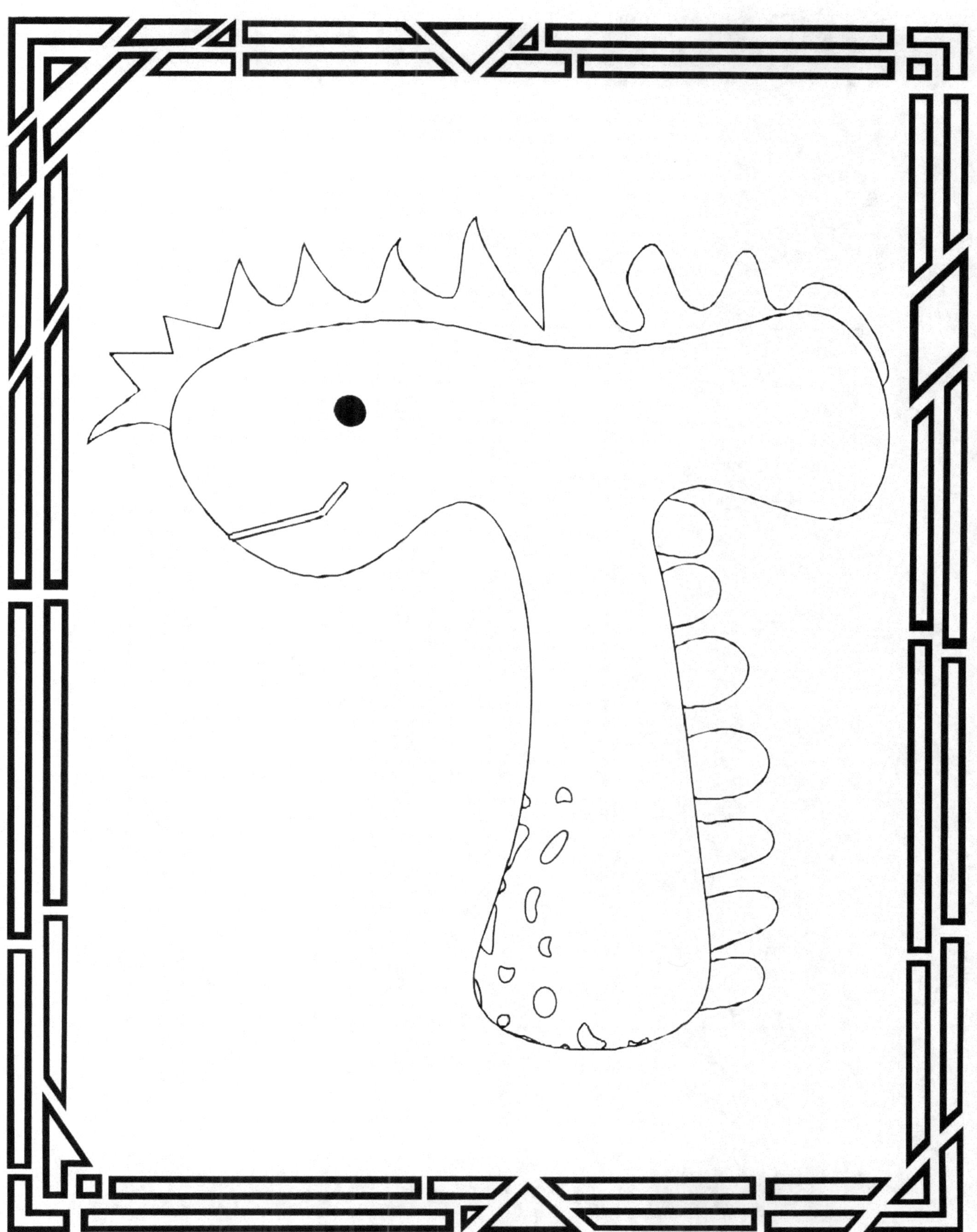

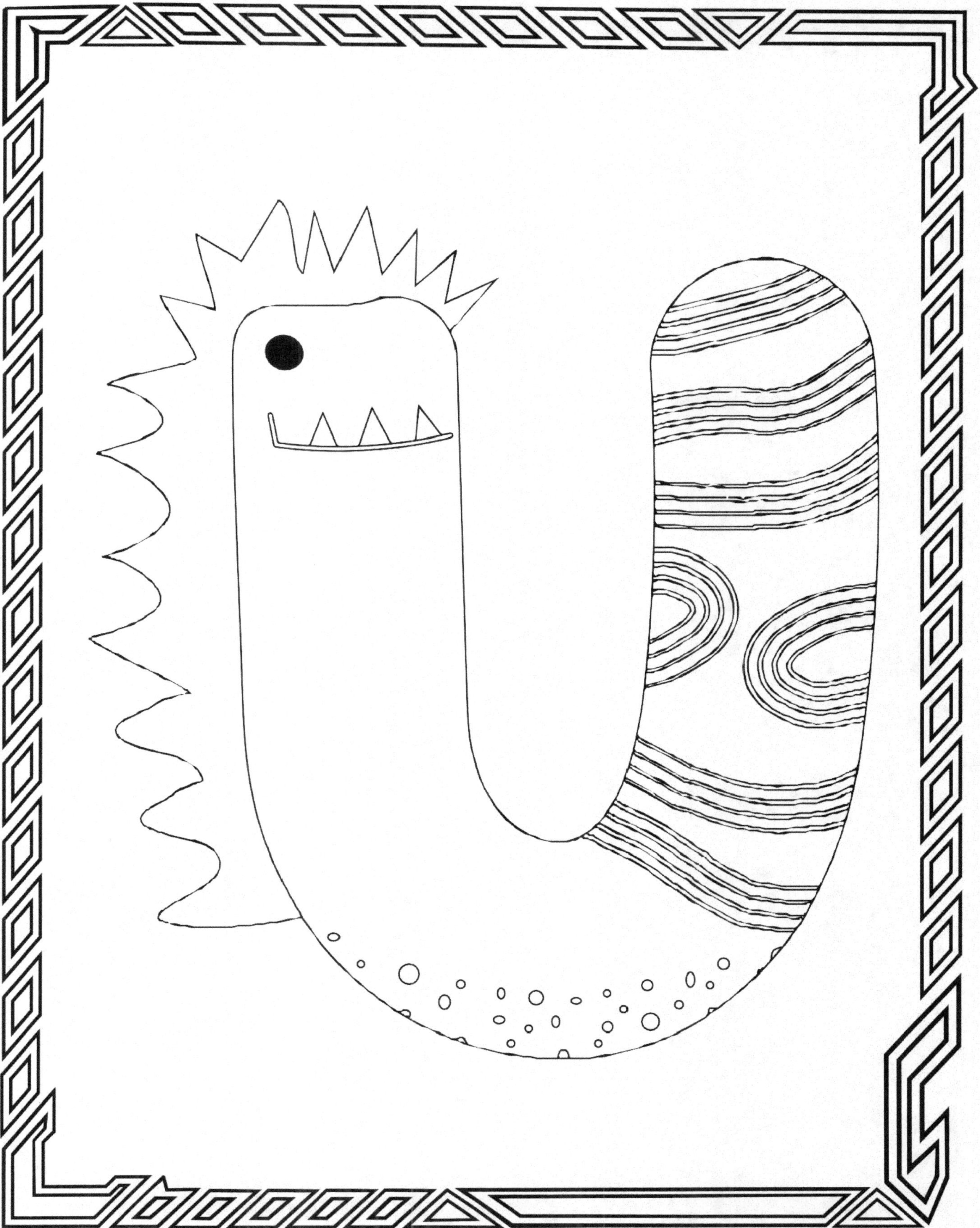

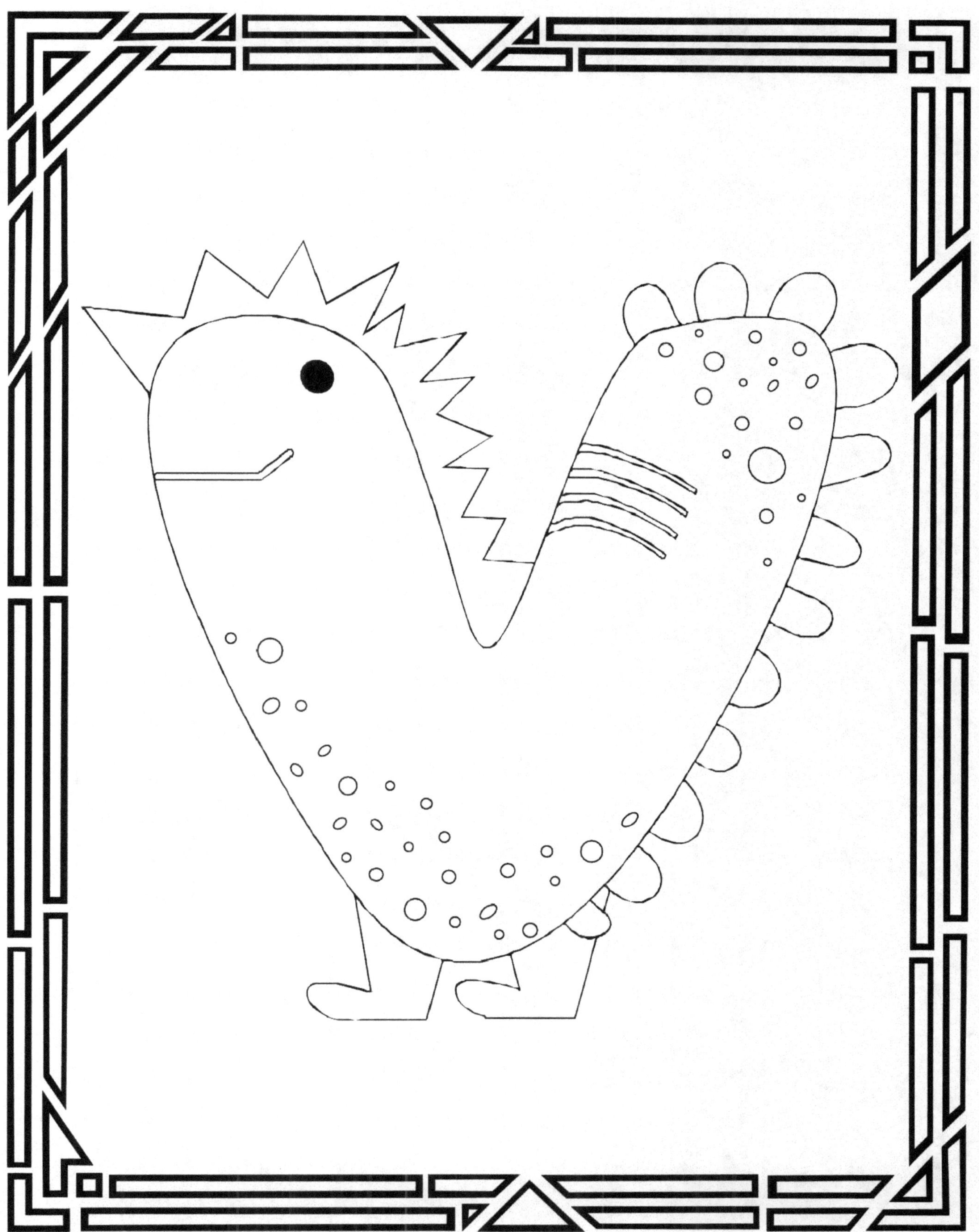

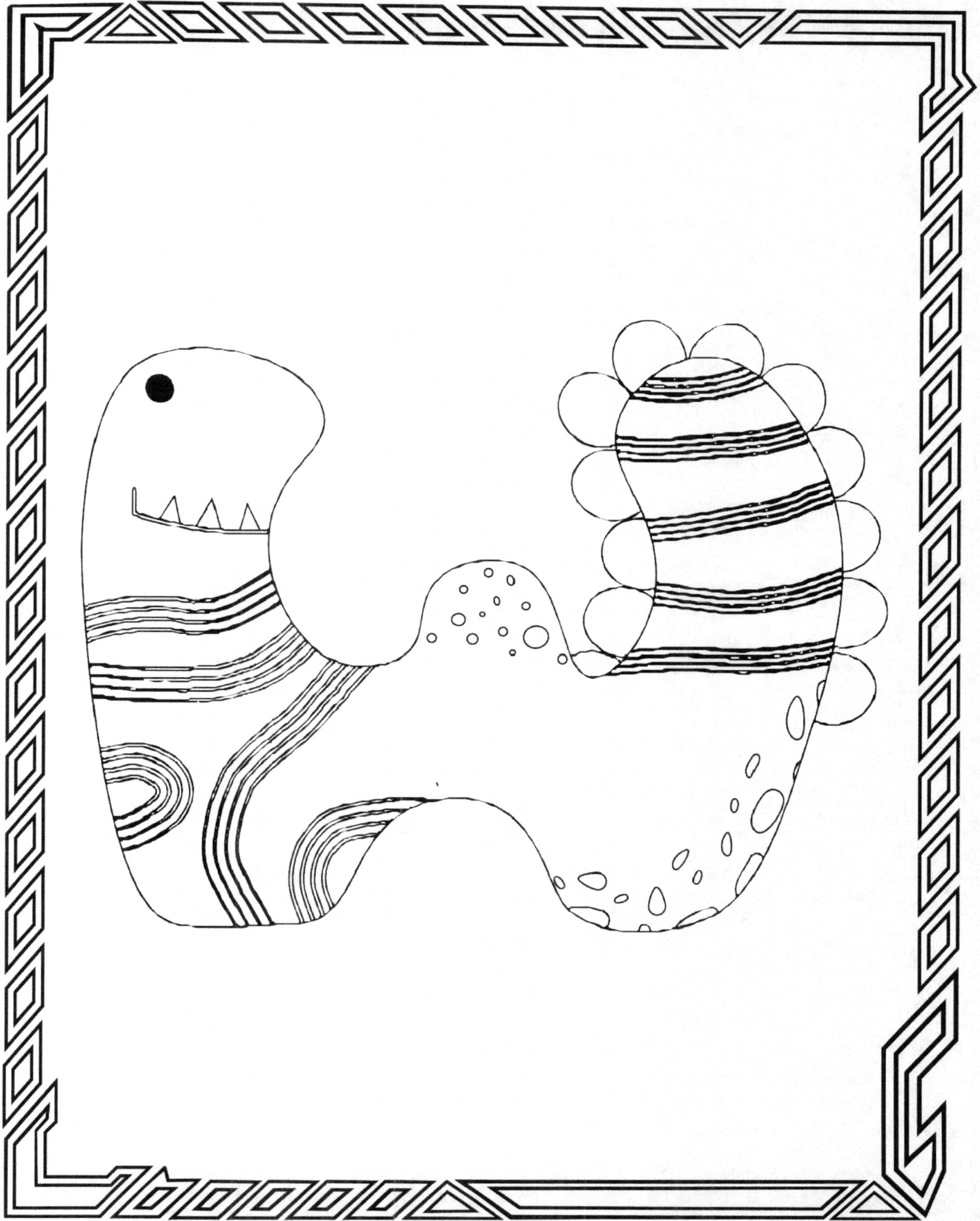

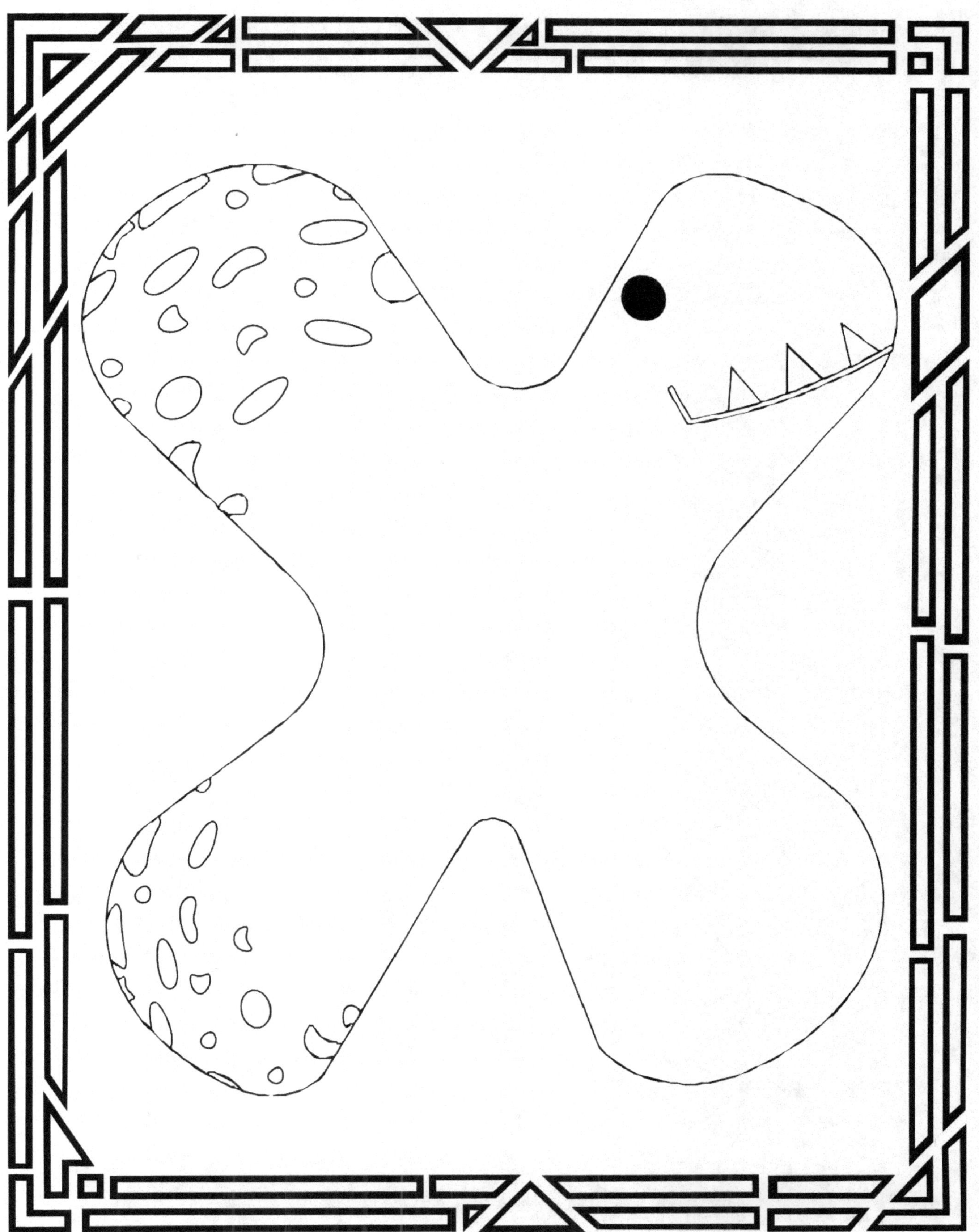

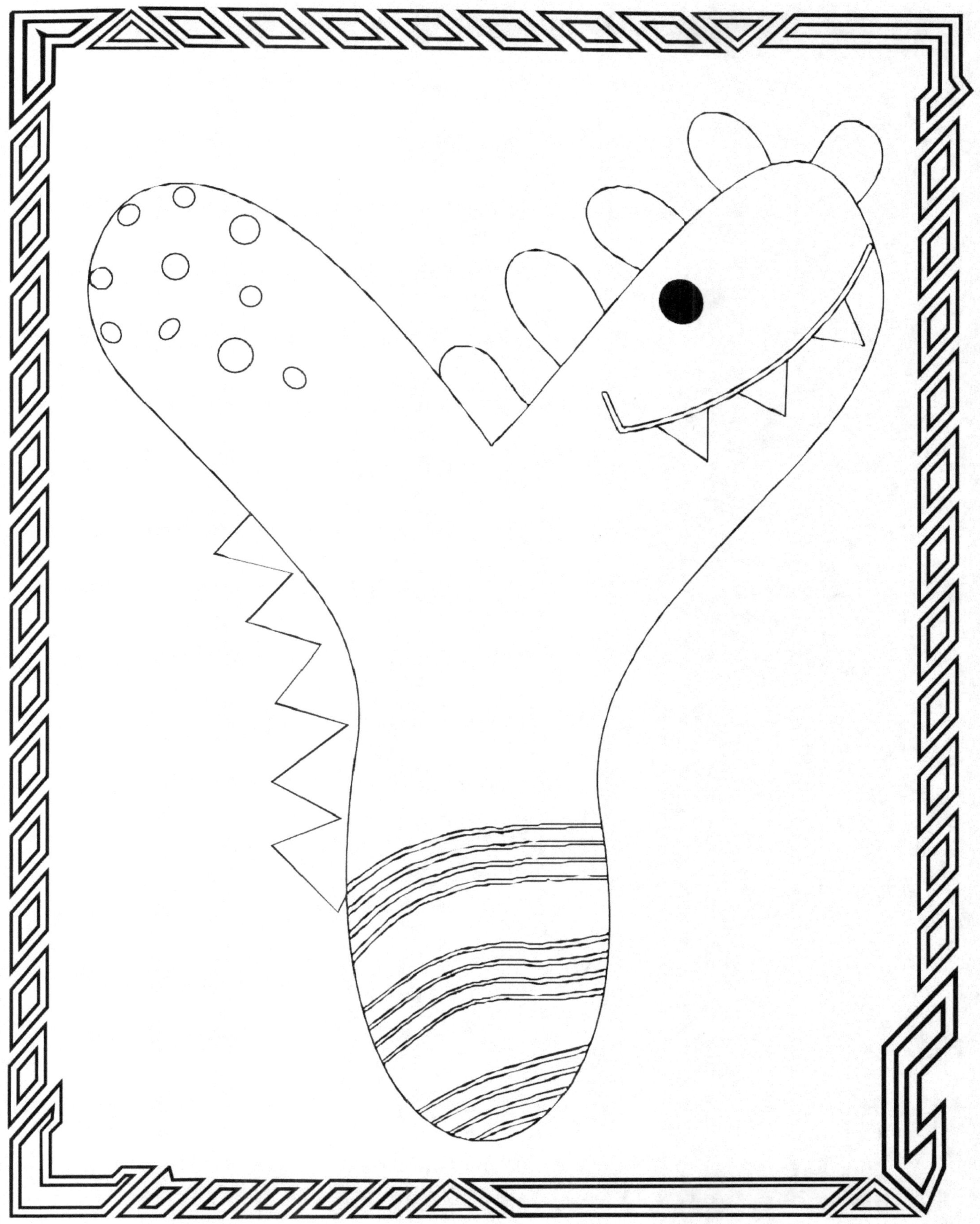

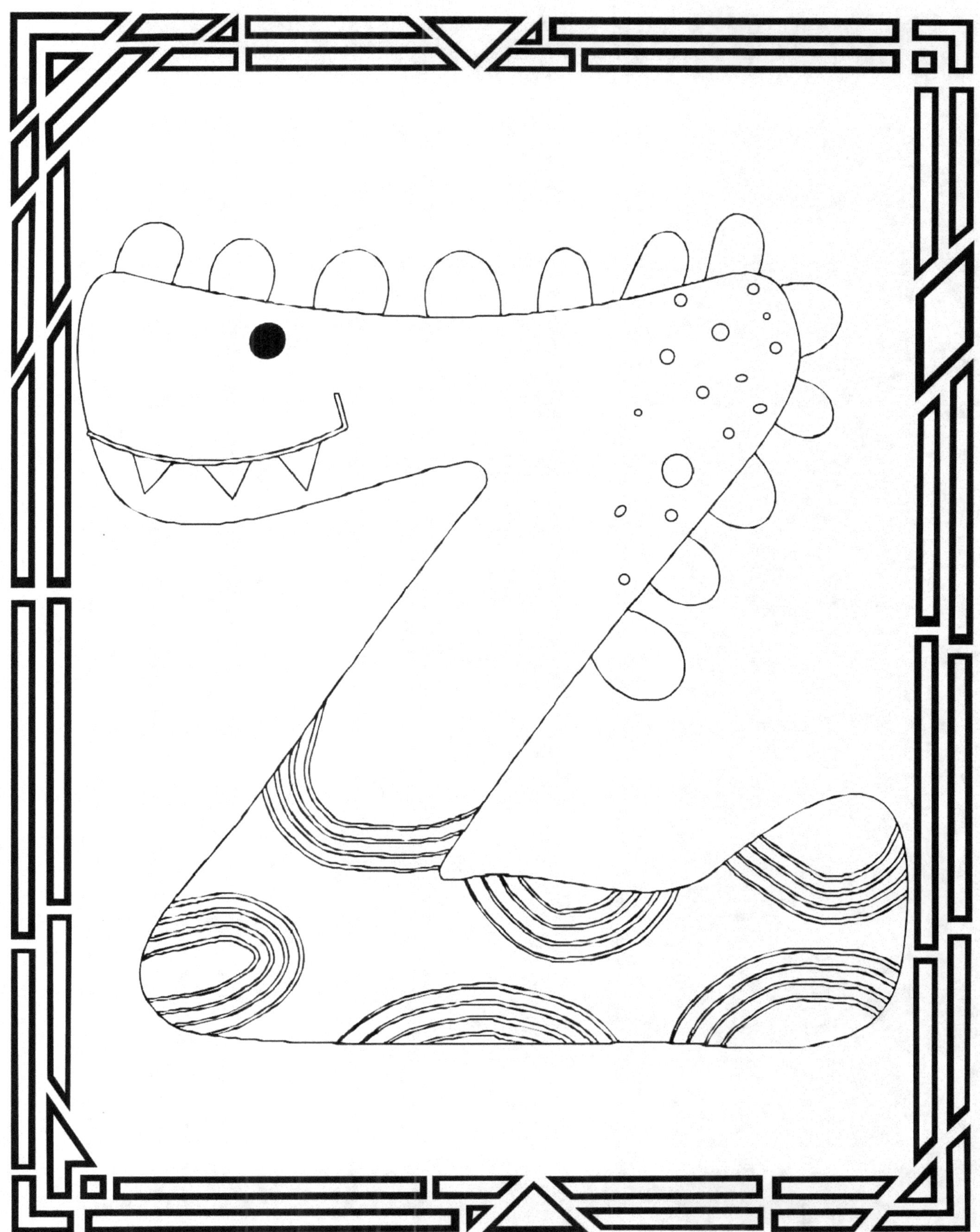

www.ingramcontent.com/pod-product-compliance
Lightning Source LLC
LaVergne TN
LVHW080818170826
845678LV00011B/2062

* 9 7 9 8 4 1 6 7 3 9 2 0 1 *